abc

Illustrated by Sarah Horne

With guidance notes for parents
at the back of the book

Aa

apple

Bb

bus

Cc

cow

Dd

dog

Ee

elephant

Ff

fish

Gg

goat

Hh

hat

Ii

ink

Jj

jam

Kk

king

Ll

lemon

Mm

moon

Nn

nest

octopus

Pp

panda

queen

Rr

rabbit

Ss

sun

Tt

tent

Uu

umbrella

Vv

van

Ww

windmill

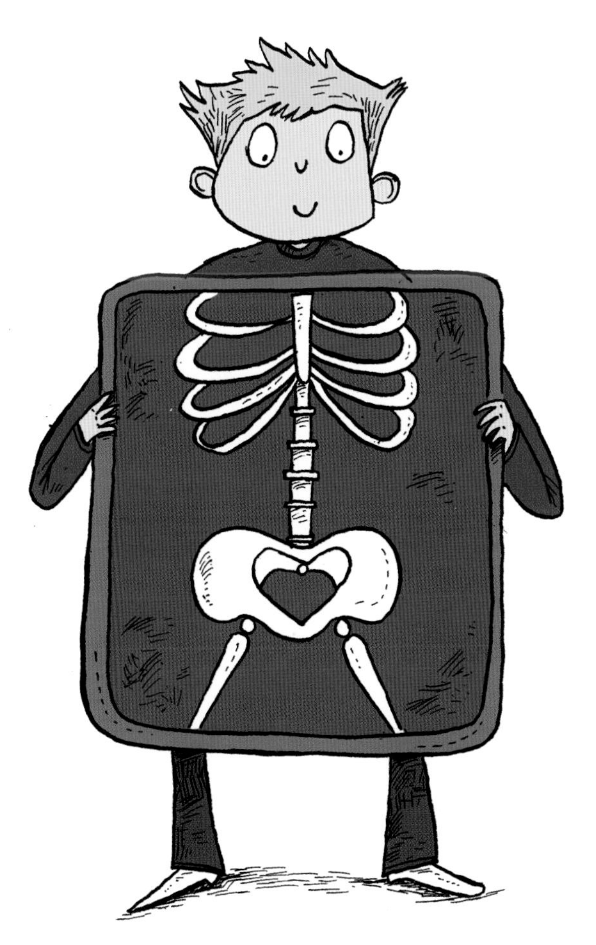

x-ray

Yy

yellow

Zz

zebra

a b c d

e f g h

i j k l m

n o p q

r s t u v

w x y z

Guidance notes

Learning the alphabet is an essential part of learning to read, and children with a good knowledge of the alphabet have a great advantage in their early reading and writing.

Letter-names and letter-sounds

These days, many children are taught to read with a **phonics** approach, using the sounds of the letters rather than their names. This book links letters to pictures based on the most common **letter-sounds** ("**i** for ink" rather than "**i** for ice cream"). You can help your child by using letter-sounds rather than letter-names. If you are not sure how to pronounce these, you can listen to them on the Very First Reading website, **www.usborne.com/veryfirstreading*** – go to the Resources area and scroll down to **Pronouncing the phonemes**.

Playing games with letter-sounds

Developing a child's awareness of letter-sounds is an important pre-reading skill, and can be fun too. Try playing "I-spy" with your child, using letter-sounds instead of letter-names.

*US readers go to **www.veryfirstreading.com**

You'll find "I spy with my little eye, something beginning with *tuh*" is much easier than "something beginning with T" for young children.

Learning letter-names

Of course, children do need to learn the letter-names at some stage. Many enjoy learning alphabet songs even before they understand what the alphabet is for. As their reading and writing become more secure, they will feel more comfortable using letter-names for spelling.

The first few letters

It's not essential to learn the letters in alphabetical order. Many children start by learning the letters in their names. Some phonics methods teach a handful of letters at a time – many begin with **s a t p i n**, which are fairly distinct from each other and allow the formation of many common words. Even if your child starts with one of these methods, they will be building up a knowledge of the alphabet, and this book will help not only to reinforce the letters they have learned but to introduce new ones too.

Editor: Mairi Mackinnon
Designed by Caroline Spatz

First published in 2011 by Usborne Publishing Ltd., Usborne House, 83-85 Saffron Hill, London EC1N 8RT, England. www.usborne.com

UE. First published in America in 2011.

USBORNE VERY FIRST READING

There are twenty-four titles in the **Usborne Very First Reading** series, which has been specially developed to help children learn to read.

To find out more about the structure of the series, go to **www.usborne.com/veryfirstreading**